Acknowledgements

The author is grateful to the following individuals: Jamie Allmund, Andrew Ashford, Shaun Cronin, John Curley, Gill Fozard, Anika Grant-Braham, Barbara Grant-Braham, Danielle Grant-Braham, Bruce Lockwood, Helen Peabody-Rolf, David Sale, Dominik Soanes and Pete Williams. Thank you also to Rod Grainger and all at Veloce Publishing, Gusto Communications, and the members of the Dorset Fire and Rescue Extrication Team.

The accompanying photographs are largely from the author's personal collection, although both the RAC and Dorset Police have also provided some: these have been acknowledged accordingly.

In researching the content, wider reading was undertaken from a variety of sources, including:

(Courtesy RAC)

British Parking Association .... www.britishparking.co.uk
British Red Cross .... www.redcross.org.uk

The Essential Driver's Handbook

What to do in the event of an accident, roadside first aid, safety tips for lone drivers & much more

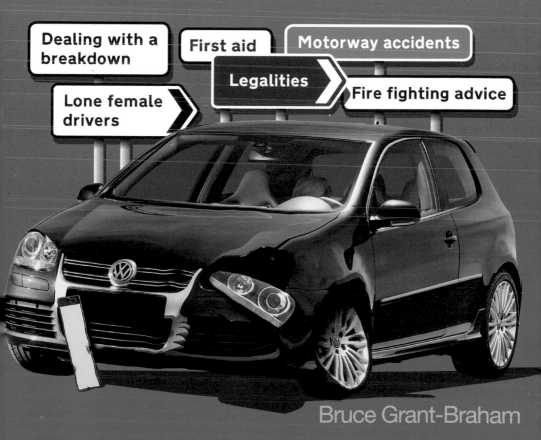

Dealing with a breakdown

First aid

Motorway accidents

Legalities

Lone female drivers

Fire fighting advice

Bruce Grant-Braham

Contents

Crimestoppers .... www.crimestoppers-uk.org
Department of Transport .... www.dft.gov.uk
DirectGov .... www.direct.gov.uk
Dorset Fire & Rescue .... www.dorsetfire.co.uk
Dorset Police .... www.dorset.police.uk
Drivers Vehicle and Licensing Authority (DVLA) .... www.dvla.gov.uk
Fire Service .... www.fireservice.co.uk
Highways Agency .... www.highways.gov.uk
The Highway Code .... www.direct.gov.uk/en/travelandtransport/highwaycode/
dg_070202
Park Mark .... www.parkmark.co.uk
RAC .... www.rac.co.uk
RAC Report on Motoring 2012 .... www.rac.co.uk/report-on-motoring/report-2012
Royal Society for the Prevention of Accidents (ROSPA) .... www.rospa.com
RTC Rescue .... www.rtc-rescue.com
St Andrew's First Aid .... www.firstaid.org.uk
St John Ambulance .... www.sja.org.uk
South West Ambulance Service NHS Foundation Trust .... www.swast.nhs.uk
Thatcham – The Motor Insurance Repair Research Centre ... www.thatcham.org
The Under 17 Car Club www.under17-carclub.co.uk
Which? Magazine .... www.which.co.uk

Glossary

BPA	The British Parking Association
CCTV	Closed circuit television
CPR	Cardiopulmonary Resuscitation
DVLA	Drivers Vehicle and Licensing Authority
GPS	Global Positioning System
HGV	Heavy Goods Vehicle
PNC	Police National Computer
ROSPA	Royal Society for the Prevention of Accidents
SatNav	Satellite Navigation
TWOC	Taking Without Owner's Consent

Dedication

This book is dedicated to Barbara, Danielle and Anika.

Introduction

One of the great freedoms of the 20th and 21st centuries has been the ability to travel largely unrestricted in your own personal transport. To be able in our society to drive to our place of work and to the shops, to take a touring holiday or a weekend excursion and to drop the children at school have all become part of our national psyche. Equally, the ability to transport goods on journeys such as from manufacturer to retailer has become a necessity for our economy, as a national priority has increasingly been given in business to road transport.

Setting out on the journey to work or taking the children to school is a part of everyday life in the UK. (Courtesy RAC)

Motoring started as an elitist activity as the original vehicles were so expensive, but as technologies improved and the costs of owning and running vehicles reduced, the general population has come to regard and accept the usage of personal transport as a right.

The popularity of vehicle usage by the UK population of approximately 63 million individuals can be gauged by the fact that in 2011 there were 42 million drivers and 36 million vehicles on our roads.

Such freedoms do, though, bring with them their own problems. A vehicle has a value, whether it be the smallest runabout or a supercar, and will in its own right be attractive to thieves. Its

Membership of an organisation that can help in the event of a breakdown, such as the RAC, provides drivers with peace of mind. (Courtesy RAC)

Many journeys take place on motorways, which are scary places to break down.

contents too might be a temptation. Occasionally the occupants themselves can be the target for robberies and assaults.

Cars are complicated pieces of equipment that need constant care and maintenance. Their reliability has improved enormously of late, but there are still instances where they breakdown. This can be through mechanical defect or, more likely, poor maintenance. The latter is always a false economy.

Unfortunately accidents occur in all fields of human activity, but where vehicles travelling at various velocities in opposite directions are concerned, road

Supercars, like this Lamborghini, are packed with sophisticated electronics. If it broke down would you be able to get it going again?

Poor maintenance causes breakdowns. Saving money in this respect is always a false economy. (Courtesy RAC)

traffic accidents can have devastating consequences. In 2009 there were 220,000 reported casualties of all severities on UK roads.

This book is intended to give practical advice for a number of the scenarios that may be encountered on the roads, whether accidental or criminal in nature. Experts from the relevant emergency services have freely given their advice, as well as validating the final manuscript. One of the intentions is that this book might help you to be prepared in the event of an incident and so minimise the consequences. Ideally, it may help you to avoid such incidents in the first place.

If you think that breaking down and being involved in an accident are remote happenings, they are not. As a member of the Guild of Motoring Writers I have driven many thousands of miles following and recording my passion for motor racing, and I have, unfortunately, been involved in both. Amongst a number of mechanical mishaps as a lone driver over the years I have had an MGB starter motor let me down in a remote part of the New Forest – and this was in the days before mobile phones. Punctures, cylinder head gasket failure, collapsed exhaust systems and

Road traffic accidents occur regularly: there were 220,000 casualties of all types in the UK in 2009.

blocked carburettor jets have all taken their toll on my patience and sanity. Yes, I have run out of fuel on a motorway too, when my car's fuel gauge was indicating half full! Unlike a pilot, you shouldn't always believe your instruments!

I am particularly indebted to Inspector Shaun Cronin of Dorset Police for all the help and encouragement he has given me, at a time when he and his force had never been busier. I first met Shaun at the scene of a road accident when he responded on behalf of Dorset Police. I had been following another car when, at speed, it unexpectedly turned on to the verge in front of me, drove along the top of a hedge, demolished a gateway, and hit head on the bank of a lane which was at right angles to the main road. The elderly driver had collapsed at the wheel and, being first on the scene, I had to put in to action many of the pieces of advice contained within chapters 6, 7 and 8 of this book. Luckily, although initially unconscious, the driver was not badly hurt, whilst his wife, a passenger, was remarkably calm considering the hair raising ride she had just been subjected to. Despite all my training I did, though, forget the obvious. When the paramedics quickly arrived the first thing one did was dip her finger in the liquid that was under the car. Luckily it was water from a ruptured radiator, but had it been fuel we might have all been in trouble. Why? In the heat of the moment I had forgotten to turn off the car's ignition!

Inspector Shaun Cronin of Dorset Police.
(Courtesy Dorset Police)

Shaun has always been passionate about road safety, and firmly believes in the education of drivers – prevention as opposed to cure you might say – and as a result he is a leading light in The Under 17 Car Club (www.under17-carclub.co.uk). The teenagers he helps to mentor are taught to drive by their parents in their own cars, in controlled

At only 13 years of age, Under 17 Car Club member Eloise proficiently drives a fifty-seater coach under supervision and on a private road.

Caterham UK supports the Under 17 Car Club with a Driving Day, and members can drive Caterham cars – but not like this!

conditions away from public roads, and with the help of the Club's instructors. A progress check is undertaken every three or four meetings. They are given first aid courses, skid pan sessions, as well as taking part in driving skills tests. Throughout the year the club holds a number of special events, including a Truck Day, a charity fundraising day, 4x4 Day, Rally Day, and a Caterham Driving Day (with Caterham UK). Such experience equips the young members with the knowledge to cope with scenarios such as are addressed in this book. Equally, it turns the members into extremely good drivers well before they eventually take their driving test.

A second individual I would particularly like to single out is John Curley of Dorset Fire and Rescue. He readily gave up his own time to help the author with the Fire Service's approach to road traffic accidents and collisions. He is particularly keen on improving techniques for rescuing individuals from crashed vehicles, and runs the Dorset Fire and Rescue Extrication Team which competes successfully in national

competitions. In furthering his ambition to improve technical methodologies he has set up his own website – RTC Rescue (www.rtc-rescue.com) – which is a respected source of specialist information and accessed by like-minded experts worldwide.

Finally, David Sale, of South Western Ambulance Service NHS Trust, who, despite a huge workload, took time out to advise me about roadside first aid as outlined in Chapter 8.

In reading this book you might end up with the impression that driving a vehicle is anything but a pleasurable experience, but that is not so. The purpose of the book is to prepare you for a variety of possible scenarios which, luckily, are mainly rare. Hopefully you will be able to avoid these scenarios if you implement just some of the advice you will read.

Above all, enjoy your driving; it is still a wonderful freedom.

Bruce Grant-Braham, PhD, Director,
Motor Sport Research Group,
Bournemouth University

John Curley (centre) with two members of his Dorset Fire & Rescue Extrication Team, and a selection of the specialist equipment required at accident scenes.

one

What to do if your car breaks down

Top tips
- Turn on your hazard warning lights
- If possible, park your car in a safe place
- On roads other than a motorway position your warning triangle appropriately
- Telephone for assistance

Useful phone numbers that you should store in your mobile phone:
The police Non-emergency (England & Wales) 101
Emergency 112 or 999
The Highways Agency: 0300 123 5000
Your Breakdown Assistance provider

No car is totally immune from breaking down. Membership of a breakdown assistance organisation will give you great peace of mind. (Courtesy RAC)

In this case the hazard warning triangle and the first aid kit may be found in the BMW's boot behind this panel.

Do you know where your vehicle's hazard warning triangle is located? Look for the triangular symbol.

Your hazard warning triangle should be placed on the same side of the road as you are to alert approaching drivers – DON'T USE IT ON MOTORWAYS.

This hazard warning triangle is too close to the car – the recommended distance is at least 45 meters (147 feet). A fluorescent jacket is sensibly being worn.

If your car suffers a mechanical breakdown on a road other than a motorway, the first thing you should do is to turn on the hazard warning lights. If the car is capable of being moved then as a matter of priority it should be parked in as safe a place as possible where it will not impede traffic flow.

Once that has been done *The Highway Code* recommends that you should then place your warning triangle "… at least 45 meters (147 feet) behind your broken-down vehicle on the same side of the road."

The only exception to this last suggestion is if you have broken down on a motorway. Don't use your warning triangle there as it is far too dangerous to be walking around, as other vehicles are travelling towards and past you at high speed.

The hazard warning triangle will additionally help identify you to potential rescuers. (Courtesy RAC)

If the breakdown has occurred in low visibility, such as mist or at night, you would be well advised to wear a fluorescent jacket or something similar to make sure that you stand out. It is sound advice in such situations to leave your car's sidelights on, too. Having turned them on, make sure that you don't obscure them, and never walk between your car and oncoming traffic (except to place the warning triangle).

Finally, ring for assistance. Your breakdown assistance organisation will want to know your location and what the problem might be. The RAC, for example, will aim to reach you within 40 minutes, 24/7, 365 days a year, and will give you priority, if you're in a vulnerable situation, such as a lone driver or a disabled driver.

What to do if your car breaks down on a motorway

Top tips
- If unable to leave the motorway or reach a service area, indicate and move to the hard shoulder
- Switch on the hazard warning lights
- Get out of your car on the passenger side
- As quickly as possible, move everyone out of the car, off the hard shoulder and onto the roadside verge/bank to await assistance. Position everyone behind a barrier if there is one
- Phone for assistance
- Do not attempt any repairs

Statistically, motorways are safer than single carriageway country roads in the UK. The problem with motorways is that

Motorway hard shoulders are very dangerous places. Those speeding lorries are very close, so never stay in your car longer than necessary.

because the average vehicle speeds are much higher, the consequences of an incident can be much greater.

Higher speed means there is less time to react to problems, and so, as a consequence, motorway driving requires a high level of alertness. It should go without saying that you should never drive when fatigued, but this is of even greater importance on a motorway.

On motorways, electronic signals over each lane provide important information to drivers. Amber flashing lights indicate hazards, temporary speed limits, dangerous driving conditions, including fog or debris, and lane closures. If the lights flash red and include an 'X' over your lane, *The Highway Code* says that, "… you must not go beyond the signal in that lane. If red lights flash on a signal in the central reservation or at the side of the road, you must not go beyond the signal in any lane." **Caution!** Before stopping, first check in the mirror, switch on the

hazard warning lights, and then draw safely to a halt.

In the event that your car develops a mechanical fault, and assuming you're able to do so, leave the motorway or turn in to the next service area. If the problem is immediate and you have to stop, pull on to the hard shoulder on the left of the carriageway. **Caution!** Remember to check the mirror first, and then signal before pulling on to the hard shoulder. Be aware that the hard shoulder is a dangerous place, and you should remain there for as little time as possible for your own safety. Park as far to the left as you can, while still leaving enough room to exit the car on the barrier side. Keeping to the left gives maximum separation from other traffic, which may include heavy lorries passing at high speed and just inches away.

If the breakdown is serious enough for you to be stranded on a carriageway, and you are unable to reach the hard shoulder, switch on the hazard warning lights as soon as possible, and only leave the vehicle to go to safety when it is absolutely safe to do so.

If possible, try to pull up next to an emergency phone – they are positioned every 1.3 miles (2 kilometers) or so; you'll save yourself a possibly lengthy – and dangerous – walk to summon assistance.

As soon as you can, even in bad weather, get everyone out of the car through the doors on the barrier side of the car: leave pets in the car. Move everyone onto the verge – ideally behind roadside barriers for added protection. It's in this kind of situation that you'll be glad you kept some rain-wear and warm clothing in the boot.

You can now summon assistance. Roadside marker posts will display an arrow which will point you in the direction of the nearest emergency phone. These are free to use, and will put you in touch with either the police or Highways Agency staff. The number of the phone will indicate to the operator exactly where you are and the direction in which you are travelling. **Caution!** While you're on the phone, keep your eyes on approaching traffic all the time, in case another vehicle skids in your direction. Mobile phones are discouraged as a means of summoning assistance by the Highway Code. Should you use one, though, the marker posts will be numbered, and so providing this information will tell the operator where you are.

In some places, driver location signs are now being introduced on near-side verges of major roads. These are designed so that they can be seen from the road whilst driving. They give location information without the need to stop. The signs have a white border with a blue background upon which are yellow letters. There are three rows of information with the top row being the number of the road, for example, 'A38.' The middle row indicates the direction

of travel, and the bottom row the distance from the notional start point of the road.

On motorways information about hazards is given via prominent coloured lights. Here, drivers are being advised of an accident ahead. (Courtesy RAC)

You should tell the operator:

Your location.
Breakdown details.
If you are travelling alone or are disabled so you get priority treatment.
Once you've completed the call, you can return to the location of your breakdown but keep well clear of the hard shoulder.

The hard shoulder is a dangerous place. Unfortunately, statistics reveal that as many as 250 people are killed on the UK's motorway hard shoulders each year whilst waiting to be rescued. Many such incidents are caused by tired drivers who have lost concentration. You should not stay on the hard shoulder any longer than is absolutely necessary, whatever the weather.

Once your problem has been resolved, if you're able to continue your journey remember the speed differential between you and the traffic already passing. **Caution!** Accelerate up to the appropriate speed on the hard shoulder before rejoining the traffic to your right. Select as long a gap as possible in the passing traffic before indicating and pulling out.

Avoiding breakdowns

Top tips
• Take precautions to avoid breaking down, such as making sure you have adequate fuel for your journey
• Familiarise yourself with your vehicle's handbook
• Regularly undertake basic vehicle maintenance checks such as checking tyres are inflated properly and not damaged

Be prepared
Mechanical vehicle breakdowns don't discriminate – they can happen at any time and to any age of car. A puncture can happen as you drive your brand new pride and joy home from the dealership. Breakdowns can also occur

Do you look closely at your car's fault-finding display before setting off on a journey? It may alert you to potential problems.

Any shortcuts in maintenance will catch you out in cold weather, so stick religiously to the car manufacturer's instructions. (Courtesy RAC)

RAC patrols have access to databases that hold the technical details of most vehicles. (Courtesy RAC)

Extreme weather increases the demands on breakdown assistance organisations. (Courtesy RAC)

at the most awkward of times and in the most inclement of weather.

There was a time, of course, when cars were mechanically simpler, when many drivers could rectify mechanical problems themselves at the roadside. Nowadays, however, cars are so complex that this is rarely the case. Who these days is sufficiently mechanically or electronically qualified to address engine management systems and their like?

The first rule is to anticipate that things can, and probably will, go wrong at some point, so join one of the major motoring organisations. Not to do so is a false economy. Such organisations boast patrol staff who possess the necessary specialist skills to get you on the move again or to take your car to the nearest garage.

There are a number of useful items you should consider keeping in your car in case you suffer a mechanical breakdown.

Checking the tyres regularly will help prevent punctures and blow outs. Could you change this wheel? Do you know where the jack is?

Do you know how to use the jack, if your vehicle still has one?

If you have such a thing do you know where the key to the locking wheel nuts is located?

Top tips
- Fully charged mobile phone
- Maps
- First aid kit
- Fire extinguisher
- Jump leads
- Tow rope
- Torch
- Spare bulbs
- Reflective triangle
- Warm / space blanket
- Reflective jacket
- Wellington boots
- De-icing equipment including an ice scraper
- Folding shovel
- Pencil and notepad

Tread depth indicator (arrowed) moulded into the tyre.

Avoiding a breakdown

To reduce the possibility of a breakdown, familiarise yourself with your vehicle's handbook, and have the vehicle regularly serviced. As one of the major motoring assistance organisations, the RAC attends about 2.5 million breakdowns a year. The most common faults that its patrols find are those caused by a lack of maintenance and/or lack of understanding of the car's systems. For example, a simple routine like checking the tyres for damage and the correct pressure, as recommended by the manufacturer, can help prevent flat tyres or – even worse – blow outs, which can make the car hard to control.

It's recommended that you familiarise yourself with some basic maintenance tasks, but, unless you're sufficiently qualified, skilled and experienced, leave the more complex jobs – such as changing sparkplugs or replacing the fan belt – to the professionals.

A good example of how breakdown analysis has assisted the motorist is the audible warning signal, available in most vehicles today, which is used to indicate

Some cars will now tell you when a full service is needed – essential to keep your vehicle running smoothly.

Make it a priority to know where the oil filler is – look for the yellow oil can symbol ...

... it will be on the top of the engine.

when lights have been left on. The large number of breakdowns and flat batteries caused by lights being left on encouraged the development of such useful devices.

Basic maintenance checks

Ensure that your vehicle is regularly serviced (consult the handbook for recommended intervals). It can be all too easy to overlook the correct service date. Some cars tell you when a service is due – do not ignore this reminder.

Examine the operation of all exterior lights to ensure they comply with legal requirements. All headlights and indicator lenses must be free from damage, such as cracks or missing glass or plastic. Remember to keep the lights clean.

Check front and rear windscreen wiper blades for wear or splitting.

Check windscreen washers, making sure that they are adjusted correctly. Appropriate screen wash additive is also recommended, especially in winter.

Ensure all dashboard warning lights operate correctly.

Check oil and coolant levels. Ensure they are topped up correctly, and have the anti-freeze content of the cooling system checked by your garage, particularly in winter.

Check the battery connections, ensuring that they are tight and free from any corrosion.

If your car still has them, inspect the jack and wheel brace, making sure you're confident about their use. If locking wheel nuts are fitted, ensure the locking key is safely stowed in the car.

It may be useful to practice changing a wheel for the spare (on a level surface), following the instructions in the vehicle's handbook. Alternatively, your vehicle may be fitted with run-flat tyres, or other systems. Whatever the system, check it out. Be aware that space saver (very narrow) spare wheels have strict speed ratings.

Tyres (including the spare, if you have one) should be checked for condition, pressure and tread depth.

Two important gauges. Fuel level (left) and engine temperature. Failing to keep an eye on these could result in a breakdown.

Breakdown assistance organisations will help you if you run out of fuel – but this is entirely avoidable. (Courtesy RAC)

23

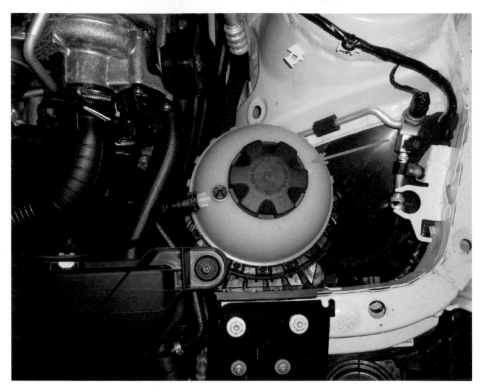

Establish where your car's cooling system can be topped up with water. Do beware of very hot steam if the engine has been running.

The current UK minimum legal tread depth for cars and light commercial vehicles is 1.6mm around the total circumference and three quarters of the width of the tyre. Remaining tread depth will be indicated visually by the built-in tread depth bars on the tyre itself. For safety, it's wise to replace the tyres when the tread depth has reduced to 3mm.

Periodically inspect the vehicle's keys for wear, and replace them if necessary. A worn key will quickly wear out a lock barrel and cause the lock to jam. It is worth noting that batteries in the fob will usually require replacement at least twice a year to maintain their operating performance.

A few self-help tips

Flat battery

If your vehicle will not start, it may well be due to a faulty battery. However, if the engine tries to turn over, the battery may not be completely dead. Check that all the electrical items, including interior or exterior lights or entertainment systems are switched off, and leave the car standing for 20 minutes. Do not try to restart your car during that period – 20 minutes is often enough to allow the battery to regain sufficient power to start up the engine. Get into the habit of turning off all controls – including lights, the heated rear window, and radio – before turning off the engine once

Changing an offside wheel puts you at risk. It's good that this car is positioned as near to the verge as possible. (Courtesy RAC)

It may be necessary to tow your car to a place of safety if you are stranded in a dangerous location. (Courtesy RAC)

Tow ropes are largely a thing of the past, and all of the breakdown assistance organisations now possess more sophisticated systems. (Courtesy RAC)

parked up for the night. This will extend the life of your battery and reduce the chance of a flat battery.

Modern car batteries are required to power many more electrical devices than even a decade ago and they take some time to fully charge. A drained battery should ideally be charged from a purpose-made charger but can be re-charged once the engine has been started by driving on the road, too. Ideally, as few electrical devices as possible should be used during the charging period of the drive, and be aware that it can take as many as 200 miles to fully charge a battery using this method. If you only drive a short distance, this will not give the battery time to recover.

Key stuck in ignition or steering lock jammed

Gently turn and wiggle the key whilst moving the steering wheel. This will often free up the key/steering lock. Sounds simple, and it is …

Air-conditioning and water 'leaks'

If you find a puddle of liquid under the car, it may well be a normal byproduct of the air-conditioning system (condensation dripping), rather than a leak from the radiator or other part of the cooling system. A genuine coolant leak will normally contain an anti-freeze additive, and will have a blue/green tint and a distinct smell. **Caution!** Do not drive a vehicle with a coolant leak;

the engine can be seriously and/or irrevocably damaged.

Automatic transmission

If you have an automatic vehicle and the engine fails to turn over when you turn the key, it's possible there is a fault with the inhibitor switch, which is installed to prevent you starting the car if the gearlever is in any position other than 'Neutral' or 'Park.' Select 'Neutral' or 'Park' several times, and then try to start the vehicle.

Remote key fob/immobiliser not operating

There has been much media coverage about radio waves blocking signals from car key fobs, and locking owners out of their cars or failing to deactivate the immobiliser. This is a genuine problem. Open the car with the physical key, get in and close the door behind you, and then retry the remote key fob when sitting in the car (This keeps out the radio waves).

Keys locked in car or lost

No fewer than 75,000 RAC members locked their keys inside their cars during 2003. Have a spare key cut and keep it in a safe place (not in the car!). If you have a 'transponder' key which sends a coded signal to the central locking, never carry the master key (often red in colour) – leave that at home and use the ones provided by the manufacturer for everyday use. The vehicle manufacturer will also be able to supply spare coded keys.

two
Carpark safety

Parts of this chapter should be read in conjunction with Chapter 4, which discusses carjacking.

Cars are vulnerable where we park them temporarily, and are nowhere near as secure as they might be if locked in the garage at home.

Top tips
- Look for carparks displaying the Park Mark® logo
- A well-lit carpark is a safer carpark
- Park close to the main entrance
- Don't allow anything with your personal details – including your address – to be visible from outside your vehicle
- Hide valuables in the boot – if you can, before you park
- Drive slowly in carparks

Both we and our vehicles can sometimes be at risk in the places where we park. Whilst assults and robberies are rare, you should be aware of the ways in which you can minimise or remove risks.

Carparks, of necessity, contain a high concentration of vehicles, which not only increases the risk of minor collisions, but is also attractive to those intent on stealing cars and/or their contents. Very rare, but there is also the potential for both muggings and assaults.

There are a number of simple precautions that can be taken to minimise both personal and vehicle risks.

Carparks management

Park Mark® carparks – which display this logo – indicate a location that is intended to deter criminal activity and anti-social behaviour.

Good advice is that you should seek out carparks where there is evidence of a proactive operational management which actively promotes and implements safety precautions. Such carparks will have obvious arrangements for:

Security
Signage
Ease of entry and exit
Internal circulation
Pedestrian movement
Disabled parking

Always look for the safest place to park

One reassurance in seeking safe parking locations is to look out for the Park Mark® Safer Parking logo. Park Mark® signs indicate a carpark that has been vetted and which has measures in place to create a safer environment for both individuals and their vehicles. You may be reassured that precautionary measures will have been built in to deter both criminal activity as well as anti-social behaviour.

Park Mark® is a prominent element of The British Parking Association's (BPA) Safer Parking Scheme, the brainchild of the Association of Chief Police Officers, and is aimed at reducing crime and the fear of crime in carparks. Independent assessors will have undertaken a risk assessment of the layout and the design of each qualifying facility, looking specifically for:

Quality management
Appropriate lighting
Effective surveillance
Clean environment

A search of the web site www.parkmark. co.uk by postcode, street name or town in the UK will reveal qualifying permanent carparks in any locality.

Much of the content of this chapter concentrates on urban locations, but you should remember that there are many other types of carpark. These include those that are temporary and arranged for major events such as sporting fixtures, festivals and carnivals. Don't completely relax your guard at these. The event organisers will mostly have been obliged to arrange stewarding and security, but the very temporary nature of the location and staff may mean they are not necessarily as secure as their permanent cousins.

Where to park?

Whatever your destination carpark, try to select a parking space that is well-lit and where there are plenty of people passing. If you can get close to the exit, shopping centre escalator, or lift, all the better, as you will have much less distance to walk and will be visible in an area of high footfall. Avoid rear or secluded entrances.

This is one way that the Park Mark® logo appears. You are strongly recommended to give preference to such carparks.

Temporary events carparks demonstrate varying levels of security. Don't let your guard down; take all the recommended precautions.

One van we might be very glad to see if we have broken down. Make it easy for the driver to find you. (Courtesy RAC)

Hide anything of value – preferably in the boot, and prior to actually arriving at the carpark (so that you're not observed doing so). Such items include

Fantastic! These car keys have the house keys attached. All the thief now needs is something with your address on ...

satellite navigation systems (sat navs) and garage door openers.

Make sure that any personal information – such as your home address – is not visible from anywhere outside the car. For the same reason, if you have to leave your car keys with an attendant, don't let them have anything with your name and address on. Why? There's a risk of identity theft and, if your house keys are attached – strongly discouraged! – illegal entrance is made that much easier. Wherever you park, try to choose a location that is well lit, has attendants and security patrols, and restricted entry and exit points.

Driver safety

If for some reason you feel particularly vulnerable and/or concerned, and there's a security presence at the carpark, ask a representative to accompany you to your car. Supermarket and shop staff are often happy to do this, too.

Consider attaching a small torch to your keyring – this is especially good in dim carparks – and also an attack alarm or piercing whistle.

Hide all your valuables, such as your sat nav, in the boot. Remember, a sucker mark on the windscreen is a clue to thieves. (Courtesy RAC)

A seaside carpark in Poole uses a novel series of illustrations to remind drivers where they parked.

Before leaving your car, make a mental note on where you have parked it, so you can quickly find your way back to it. In multi-storey carparks there are usually well signed aisles, so note down their numbers or letters and take bearings from the exit. In large carparks specifically created for events place a marker on your aerial – if your car still has one – to make it easier to find your car in amongst all the others. A used fizzy drink bottle is a personal favourite.

Be aware that locations such as station carparks will indicate to carjackers and others that the car's owners will be away for most of the day. A carparking ticket displayed as required on the dashboard will even give an idea of what time you think you may return!

Security cameras

Closed circuit television (CCTV) security cameras will go some way to preventing thefts, robberies and assaults and should be accompanied by prominent signage making everyone aware that video surveillance is being used. Perpetrators do not like the possibility of being observed so such a system may go some way to deterring them. Don't completely relax your other precautions as CCTV is not always a total deterrent.

A simple technique to enable you to find your car in a large carpark. Attach something convenient to your radio aerial.

My personal preference is for a used plastic bottle. It has done me good service at many motor racing events.

Some criminals identify where the blind spots are. Professionals also wear clothing – hoodies, dark glasses and golf caps – to make their identification that much more difficult at a later date.

Safety tips for driving in carparks

Driving too fast in carparks can cause avoidable accidents, so treat the location as you would the road outside. It may be tempting to race to that elusive vacant space, but this can mean you fail to notice pedestrians loading their cars and could also cause a road rage incident with another driver. Turn on your car's headlights if the carpark is dark, and be aware of pedestrians, especially as they may be pushing shopping trolleys or baby buggies. Always drive slowly in carparks – where elderly shoppers, distracted parents and unaware and unpredictable children are commonplace – and use your car's indicators to make other drivers and pedestrians aware of your intentions.

CCTV cameras are useful deterrents to thieves, but, if they are fixed, 'blind spots' can be readily identified.

A better solution in some locations are cameras that can traverse. Nobody then is quite sure which way they are pointing.

three
Safety tips for lone drivers

This chapter should be read in conjunction with chapters 2 and 4: carpark safety and carjacking.

Top tips
• Always lock your car's doors when driving

Breaking down in a remote location is a worrying situation. Lock yourself in, phone your breakdown assistance organisation, and resist approaches from 'Good Samaritans.'

• Carry a fully-charged mobile phone with you
• Plan your route
• Keep a map with you
• Make sure your car is mechanically sound and appropriately fuelled
• Membership of a national breakdown organisation will give reassurance

Useful phone numbers that you should store in your mobile phone:

The police: Non-emergency (England &Wales) 101; Emergency 112 or 999
The Highways Agency: 0300 123 5000
Your Breakdown Assistance provider ...

Whilst the UK's roads are mainly safe, they aren't totally risk-free. There is a very small potential for lone drivers to be more prone to both robbery and/or assault than when a car boasts several occupants and where there is, therefore, security in numbers. It's wise, therefore, to make some elementary precautions part of your everyday driving routine so you are prepared should you end up in a situation where you are totally on your own.

The first piece of advice is to try to avoid becoming stranded in the first place by making sure your car has the appropriate amount of fuel for the journey. It's quite possible, for example, to make a journey along a route that hasn't been driven for a while only to find that expected petrol stations in long remembered locations are now closed. Keeping the tank filled will avoid reliance on a petrol station which may no longer be there, or may even have changed its opening hours.

Some fuel gauges tell you how far you can go on the fuel available. Fill up well before, in this case, 124 miles!

Breakdown organisations will help you if you run out of petrol, but good preparation will prevent you being in such a situation. (Courtesy RAC)

Next, make sure your car is always mechanically sound by having it regularly serviced as recommended by the manufacturer. Even then, before a journey, particularly to a relatively remote location or just along a motorway – where the engine may be subjected to higher speeds for longer than normal – ensure that you have at least double-checked the oil and coolant levels.

Plan your road trip in advance, as you don't want to put yourself at risk by having to stop to ask for directions. Decide which major roads you are going to use and factor in fuel stops, too.

Make sure your Satellite Navigation system (SatNav) is charged up and fully operational, but don't just rely on that alone. As an aside, make sure that you regularly update your SatNav's

mapping – usually via the internet – so that and the internal map is always up to date with changes to existing roads. Many motorists never do this, and then wonder why they get lost! If you think that roads never change, the consumer magazine *Which?* found that 15% of roads change every year, whether this be in the form of new roads or changes to existing roads. Carry an up-to-date road map so you can still cope if your SatNav fails for whatever reason.

Avoid going into areas you don't know after dark – particularly urban areas. If you were to get lost it may become obvious to observers, and your chances of becoming a target for assault and carjacking could increase

Before setting off make sure you tell someone when and where you are

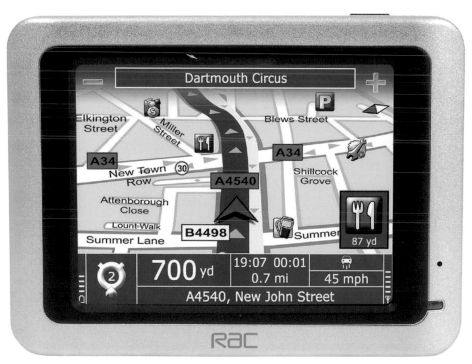

Set up your sat nav for your journey so you are less likely to get lost. Keep a road map in the car as back-up. (Courtesy RAC)

going so that, if you're overdue, the alarm can be raised or they can come and search for you. Give the people you are going to visit an estimated time of arrival and tell them which route you plan to take.

If the unexpected happens and the car develops a fault, make for the nearest garage or emergency phone to summon assistance as soon as possible. Do not plough on in the hope that the fault will cure itself, as it is quite likely that you'll make the situation worse and, as a result, be more likely to become stranded.

In a breakdown situation, wherever you are, you want to be able to summon assistance, so a mobile phone (along with a suitable in-car charger) is essential. It should always be within reach, but make sure it is kept in its holder or has a Bluetooth connection so you can use it hands-free. If your phone operates on the pay-as-you-go system, make sure the credit is topped up.

Lone women drivers

Whilst the advice in this chapter is aimed at all motorists, it is undoubtedly the case that lone female drivers often feel themselves to be more vulnerable than men.

If this is you, and your car does suffer a mechanical breakdown, the best advice, if you can, is to park in a safe location, and lock yourself inside whilst awaiting assistance. If you're on a motorway, however, remaining on the hard shoulder is very dangerous, so

If your car breaks down, lock yourself in and await assistance from your breakdown assistance organisation.

you should evacuate the car and shelter a distance away on the verge, ideally behind a crash barrier. Don't forget to take your car keys with you.

Contact your breakdown organisation as soon as possible and let them know that you are a lone female driver. They will give you priority status.

Unfortunately, you have to treat all 'Good Samaritans' as guilty until proven innocent. If a man stops and offers you unsolicited help, it's best to decline. If you're really suspicious tell him that, "It won't be long until my partner gets here," or that, "My emergency breakdown service is less than five minutes away." If really worried, you might call the police or the Highways Agency for help. Carrying a charged mobile phone with you is, therefore, very important.

Being followed

If you fear that you're being followed, what should you do (and not do)? First, do not try to race away, as this can endanger both you and other road users. Nor should you stop and confront the person you believe is following you, as this might expose you to physical risk.

The driver of the following car might flash their headlights to try to get you to stop, but don't. They may try to indicate to you that there is a problem with your car and that you should pull over. If your car is obviously performing normally, you should resist the temptation to stop.

It could, of course, be a police car that is flashing you. A marked police car will show its blue lights, though, and may sound its siren. If this is the case, you should be prepared to stop in a safe position and indicate your intentions to do so. Use your common sense, and ask yourself, "Do the police actually want me to stop or are they just trying to get past?"

Tell your breakdown assistance organisation if you are a lone female driver or disabled and it will prioritise its response. (Courtesy RAC)

Don't, at this stage, get out of the car or unlock the doors until you have spoken to the police officer and established their identity by asking to see their identification. This should also be your policy where an unmarked police vehicle might be used. Be especially careful if the officers are not in uniform – this would be an unusual situation, though, and the officers will normally be keen to establish their lawful identity to you.

The recommended solution if you are being followed and are suspicious

Being followed is very concerning, particularly if you are a lone female driver. (Courtesy RAC)

NEVER phone on the move like this. ALWAYS use a hands-free system or stop and lock yourself in before phoning for assistance. (Courtesy RAC)

is that you should not drive to your home, but instead to the nearest police station and summon assistance. Alternatively, you can call the police on your hands-free mobile phone to let them know what is happening, giving them as much detail about the following car as possible. If you're near a busy shopping area, stop and draw attention to yourself by sounding the horn, and tell appropriate bystanders what the problem is.

What else should I carry with me?
A personal attack alarm may help in certain situations, and will certainly help attract attention if you feel threatened. Keep it to hand and make sure it goes with you should you get out of the car.

Some car alarms also operate as a personal alarm.

A torch with charged batteries would be useful for situations that might occur after dark, making it possible to pick out anybody coming towards your vehicle.

Make sure you have sufficient small change in your pocket to be able to make calls from public telephone call boxes where necessary or alternatively make sure you have the relevant phone cards.

Finally, it is good advice, particularly in urban areas, to take off high-value jewellery and watches while driving as these have been known to attract attention and to increase the potential, albeit remote, for robbery.

four
Carjacking

Top tips
- Always lock your car doors whilst driving
- Never leave your car keys in the ignition whilst outside the car
- If threatened in any way, hand over your keys
- Stay alert and be especially wary at night
- Don't let down your guard – even when just outside your home
- Whenever possible, don't drive alone
- Be suspicious of minor rear-end collisions

Useful phone numbers that you should store in your mobile phone:
The police: Non-Emergency (England &Wales) 101; Emergency 112 or 999
Your insurance company
The Highways Agency: 0300 123 5000

What is carjacking?

According to Home Office statistics there are approximately 3000

carjackings in the UK each year, with approximately a third of these being in the London Metropolitan Police area.

The carjacker's prize – car keys! There is now no need to smash side windows and hot wire your car. They can simply drive away.

In the context of the millions of car journeys undertaken every day this is actually a tiny number.

Because carjacking is a potential emergency situation, even though the risk is very low, this book needs to advise not only how to avoid becoming a victim of carjacking in the first place, but also to suggest what to do in the unlikely event that you might be affected.

Carjacking is the forcible theft of a car by any means, and, whilst there are relatively few carjackings in the UK each year, it can be violent and may occasionally involve a weapon.

Carjackers often use both force and fear to steal cars. Sometimes the driver is seized and pulled out of their seat to be left by the side of the road. In some high profile cases carjackers have driven off with children still in the back seat, adding extra trauma to both them and the parent left behind.

Carjacking is, therefore, a potentially traumatic experience which will leave most victims badly shaken at the very least. It can leave some victims feeling very nervous about continuing to drive.

A car might be a carjacking target because of its value. Less likely, although it happens, cars may be carjacked by individuals who are either planning a robbery or are fleeing from the scene of a crime. Sometimes carjackers are just looking for thrills. Carjackers are mostly opportunistic and often don't have specific victims in mind when they set out.

Why has carjacking increased?

Ironically carjacking has increased because of improvements in built-in car security. An unlocked car that is not immobilised is relatively easy prey for the carjacker as advances in both car alarms and locks have made

If distracted and you get out of your car, having left the keys in the ignition, carjackers can jump in and just drive away your car.

parked and locked vehicles much more difficult to steal. Computerised ignition switches, steering wheel locks, engine immobilisers and vehicle trackers are now commonplace, and have proved a serious deterrent to the traditional car thief. Additionally, carjacking usually yields undamaged cars for the thief; which is a bonus, as is having possession of the keys. The lack of a smashed window, often a by-product of a traditional car theft, means that such a car will not attract attention whilst being driven away.

Some locations where the risk of carjacking increases:

Urban areas
Commercial areas
Junctions, especially those with traffic lights
Large multi-storey carparks
Cash machines
Pay phone boxes
Drive-through take-away restaurants
Petrol stations
Car washes
Where you park at home
Recycling centres
Parking areas for dog walks

How to deter carjacking

Some simple prevention techniques can minimise the risk.

Approaching your car

Walk towards your car purposefully whilst remaining alert to what's going on around you. Make sure you have your car keys ready in your hand, and before unlocking the doors, look around to make sure there aren't any suspicious people in the vicinity. If someone comes up to you, maybe requesting advice, be wary, and watch out for potential accomplices. Be suspicious of people just sitting in their cars.

If you're loading shopping or looking after children, don't put the keys in the ignition until the last moment. Try to change your habits so that you open the car door, get in quickly, and then lock the car's doors behind you.

A new variation on the carjacking theme is the use of a simple distraction technique – a piece of paper! This is placed on the rear window. If you haven't already spotted it once you have got in to your car, locked the doors and started the engine, the carjacker will hope that you now notice in the rear-view mirror that there's a piece of paper stuck to the rear window. As this is blocking your visibility you may instinctively put the gears into neutral and get out of the car to remove it. As you vacate the driving seat the hidden carjacker leaps out from cover, gets into the driving seat and drives off. You may have 'helpfully' left the engine running, and may even have left valuables inside your car.

The advice here is, now that you are aware of such a scenario, don't wait, but drive off to a safe place before removing any pieces of paper. When you do stop, turn off the engine and take your car keys with you.

We all have a sixth sense. If your instincts tell you to be suspicious and you feel something is not right, quickly open the car door, climb in, lock the door behind you, and drive away. If you are outside the car, and don't feel personally threatened, walk away quickly.

Whilst driving

Car doors should be kept locked at all times. Some cars have an automatic locking system built in that will operate after a few seconds and once the car is moving, and these will do the work for you. That such systems exist should indicate to you the potential risks worldwide of carjacking. Keep

An option, when driving, is to lock your car doors for security. Self-locking is now a common feature on some cars.

the windows closed. If you have air-conditioning this is easy, but if the climate is such that you need to lower the windows make sure it is only by a small amount.

When stopped in traffic always allow space for an escape route in situations where you feel trouble might occur. A space equivalent to the length of one car should be sufficient. If you are unable to drive away from a threatening situation, deliberately attract attention to yourself by sounding your car's horn or shouting. Be noisy, and, if at all possible, stay in your locked car.

Try not to drive alone, and ideally team up with a passenger – an added bonus of some work-provided car share schemes. This last piece of advice particularly applies at night, but may be useful in threatening situations at any time.

Keep your purse, handbag or other valuables out of sight whilst driving, as it is surprising what can be spotted from the pavement. If you drive a convertible, don't leave any property – especially a handbag – on the seats, as it is easy for these to be grabbed from outside if you're stopped in traffic.

Don't be tempted to pick up hitch-hikers or to stop to help someone who apparently has a broken-down car.

Hide your belongings. A window left open or a convertible car provide irresistible opportunities for thieves.

This may conflict with your personal wish to be a Good Samaritan, but, unfortunately, both can be lures who may well have hidden accomplices. For the same reasons, ignore any stranger who tries to flag you down for no apparent reason. If your instinct to help is very strong where an apparent breakdown is concerned you can phone the police or the Highways Agency to get help sent. Remember, though, not to use your mobile phone while driving unless it is hands-free.

The bump and carjack

Potential carjackers sometimes engineer a minor collision, often from behind, which initially makes them appear to have accidentally hit your car. Their intention is to get you to step out of the car, and to leave your keys in the ignition. Whilst you are distracted they hope to steal the car and its contents.

If such a collision occurs, and you are suspicious, despite your instincts it may be better to remain securely in your car. You should remember that if involved in a collision or accident you are legally obliged to exchange contact and insurance details, and this can be done without getting out of the car. You should resist getting out, and, as an alternative you might lower your window slightly to converse with the other driver. Alternatively, it might be better to wave at the other car to follow you to a secure well-lit area – a garage or a police station where there are other people around. Should you then get out of your car make sure you take your car keys with you, along with any valuables, such as your wallet. You should note the other car's registration number and inform the police so that you are not subsequently accused of leaving the scene of an accident, albeit minor.

Beautiful though it is, showing off your jewellery is unwise in public, and potential carjackers may spot your hand on the steering wheel, too.

Carjackers like remote locations where there are likely to be few witnesses, and where their escape will be relatively easy.

At the petrol station

Make sure that you remove the keys and lock your doors whilst you go to the cashier to pay. Leaving the car door open, especially in petrol stations with a large number of pumps, gives a carjacker the opportunity to snatch valuables.

At your destination

Always try to park in well-lit places, ideally adjacent to the pavement. Where possible, avoid a location without a clear view, such as immediately behind a skip, alongside dense vegetation or near a large lorry. You need to be alert and able to see around you, because carjackers like the element of surprise.

If you are a woman driving on your own, make use of valet parking if available, or a carpark or garage with an attendant.

Once you are out of the car make sure all the seats are cleared of any valuables – leave nothing tempting in view. Valuables should ideally not be left in the vehicle, but if they are, they should be placed in the boot and out of sight. At all times make sure that you are alert and aware of your surroundings.

If you are a victim of carjacking

Whilst emphasising that the likelihood of being the victim of a carjacking is statistically very small, it is wise to be prepared.

Should a carjacker physically threaten you, neither resist nor argue. A car can be repaired or replaced, but

The bump and carjack is a distraction technique to get you out of your car before it's stolen and driven away.

physical damage to you is a much more unwanted situation. You should leave the area by the quickest route whilst also making a note, mental or otherwise, of any distinguishing features of the carjacker.

You should contact the police (112 or 999) to report the crime as soon as is possible, giving as good a description of the carjacker as you can.

You should, as a minimum, try and memorise the following about the carjacker and any accomplices:

Gender
Age
Race
Hair
Style of dress

In addition the details of any vehicle the carjackers might have used in the crime:

Vehicle registration number
Make
Model
Colour

What should I do if my car is stolen?
You should contact both the police and your insurance company

Police
Tell the police:
Location details
Who you are and who the registered owner of the vehicle is, if it is not you
Where and when the incident took place
Vehicle registration number
Make

Model
Colour

In immediately reporting the theft to the police, they, in turn, will submit the details to the Police National Computer (PNC).

The police will give you a reference number for the crime, which will be needed by your insurance company, and by the DVLA if you subsequently need to ask for any vehicle tax to be refunded.

At the time of writing, in law there are several different levels of carjacking offences which are covered by the Theft Act of 1968, including Taking Without the Owner's Consent (TWOC).

Insurance company
Do make sure you have an insurance policy that covers carjacking; not all do. Contact your insurer as soon as possible and obtain advice.

How can I help in the recovery of my vehicle if it is stolen?
One of the best pieces of advice is to fit a Thatcham-approved GPS tracking system, which makes the task of recovery for the police much easier.

What does Thatcham mean? In 1969 The Motor Insurance Repair Research Centre, or 'Thatcham' as it is widely known, was set up and funded by British insurers. A not-for-profit organisation, Thatcham researches ways of reducing the cost of motor insurance claims. The fitting of Thatcham-approved devices and products to your vehicle will often yield preferential insurance company quotations.

five

Road rage

The RAC Report on Motoring 2012 indicated that in the UK," ... motorists consider themselves law abiding, but worry about other motorists' annoying and potentially dangerous bad habits."

Most of us want to drive safely to our destination, giving due regard to the conditions, but there are also those who are prone to hurry and who are aggressive in their driving

21st century motoring can at times be full of frustrations. (Courtesy RAC)

style. 'Road rage' manifests itself in a number of ways, but it is typified by an angry confrontational situation involving gestures, hazardous driving and possibly the use of physical aggression.

Although relatively rare in the overall context of motoring, such situations have increased as roads have become more overcrowded and drivers more frustrated as a result. Amongst the causes of road rage are bottlenecks, selfish drivers, erratic cyclists and pedestrians. Additionally, loud music, sounding the horn, manoeuvring without indicating, overtaking and undertaking in dangerous locations, speeding and tailgating can be triggers, too.

It's possible that such behaviour mirrors many people's hectic, stressful and pressurised lifestyles, but in most cases it is purely bad driving and impatience that is the root cause. Elsewhere you can cool off in private if you get angry, but in a car the road rage driver feels anonymous, and is housed inside a heavy vehicle in which they feel isolated and protected. What's worse is that their car can be used as both a physical threat and a weapon.

Road rage involves all genders and ages, and it is most common in congested locations, such as towns and cities. Worryingly, most of us have experienced road rage at one time or another, so, amongst other things, check that you have a car insurance policy that covers road rage, as by no means all do.

What to do if confronted

Top tips
- Don't retaliate
- Avoid eye contact
- Don't gesticulate
- Avoid conflict
- Give the angry driver plenty of space

You look ahead and behind and realise the queue of traffic you are in appears endless.

It's dusk, it's winter, it's raining, you want to get home, the traffic lights are at green and still you aren't moving. (Courtesy RAC)

Avoiding eye contact with a road rage driver is advised to help defuse such a situation. (Courtesy RAC)

If you find yourself in a road rage situation the first rule is not to retaliate, as this can only inflame the situation. If possible let the aggressive driver get on with whatever they are doing, and leave them plenty of room. Don't take the situation personally, as, more than likely they're solely reacting to genetic instinct.

Avoid looking at the angry driver, as this can only increase their level of indignation and appear to be insulting them. Instead, even though they may be glaring, look ahead, drive on and find a separate route away from harm. If appropriate, find a safe parking place and calm down before restarting your journey.

Whatever you do don't make gestures or shout back – it can only escalate the situation – but grip the wheel and drive on. Tell any of your passengers to refrain from joining in with their 'observations.'

Resist sounding your horn or flashing your lights, as this can only exacerbate the situation, and you don't know how violent the angry driver might suddenly become.

In the very unlikely event that you find yourself being followed, there's a possibility that you could be subjected to a violent confrontation. Don't drive home but go straight to a police station or public place if you can. Don't race away trying to escape and evade, as you might endanger yourself and other road users.

If a face-to-face confrontation is unavoidable, don't get out of the car, but insist the other party comes to you. Lock the car's doors, partially wind down the window, and try to remain both polite and well-mannered.

Are you immune from road rage yourself? If not check out the prevention techniques.
(Courtesy RAC)

- Learn to control your emotions
- Recognise it's not personal
- Count to ten, to de-tense
- Listen to relaxing music
- Don't drive when tired

The fact that you're reading this book suggests that you're a thoughtful driver who wants to learn more about driving safely. However, could you actually be a road rager?

If the answer to any of the following questions is positive, you're demonstrating at least one of the symptoms of being a potential road

---

Preventing road rage in oneself

Top tips
- Plan ahead and leave plenty of time for your journey

rager. It also reveals that you are occasionally aggressive behind the wheel and possess the potential to be a danger on the road:

I tailgate and flash my lights at drivers who hog the wrong lane
I race to work, sometimes breaking the speed limit
I sound my horn when other drivers annoy me
I curse and shout at other drivers, even though they cannot hear me
I weave from lane to lane, often undertaking, as other drivers are so slow

Road rage is not a premeditated activity as it occurs on the spur of the moment, and nobody sets out with the intention of deliberately annoying you. It could be that, in getting angry, you are reacting to another's mistake or naivety – something we have all done. It's not personal, and so is it, therefore, really necessary to retaliate?

If you're getting tense – the time for your appointment is ticking away, for example – take some deep breaths and, if necessary, park and stretch for a few minutes. Recognise that being late is not a crime and the person you are visiting will understand.

Plan ahead and leave early, so that you're not tempted to race against the clock. Get used to adding an extra ten minutes to every journey, as this will help allow you to buy fuel or avoid congestion.

You won't have to take risks to make up time. You'll also be much calmer when you arrive, and your day will run much more smoothly. Use the travel information services on the TV and internet to see if there are any advance warnings or existing delays on your proposed route, and be prepared to find an alternative.

In reality, if you react angrily to other drivers, are you actually going to change their driving style? Being a vigilante will not work, and, on reflection, is your own driving always perfect?

If you feel yourself getting angry, try holding back briefly and count to ten, take some deep breaths and let your anger subside. Why not change what you're listening to as you drive? Relaxing music won't hype you up and will reduce stress. Classical music, or even a good comedy programme, will help remove the potential for road rage and stress.

We've all seen the road safety signs "Tiredness Kills," but lack of sleep also contributes to road rage. Have you had enough sleep? We all get tetchy if we haven't, and some say we need at least eight hours. We need to be rested, otherwise we'll be irritable and our tolerance levels of others' behaviour will be lower. Try to take a rest at least every three hours on a long trip.

Do remember that whilst you cannot influence other drivers around you, you can take charge of how they affect you.

six
Road accidents

A car submarines underneath a bus in front of you and there is an unconscious casualty. What could you do to help? (This is a training exercise.)

What should I carry in my car to cope with a car accident?

Top tips
- High visibility jacket
- Torch
- Warning triangle
- Map
- Mobile phone
- Basic First Aid kit
- Fire extinguisher

Roads frequently have to be closed to allow the emergency services to work safely at the accident scene and during subsequent investigation.

Wear a high visibility jacket or vest to make you as visible as possible. Even in daylight and perfect weather conditions you still need to be seen by other motorists who may be distracted or who are 'rubbernecking.' Many accidents happen at night and in rain or fog when visibility is doubly important. For night incidents, a fully-charged torch is of great help. Most importantly, you should not take the risk of becoming a casualty.

Turn on your car's hazard warning lights, and then, if safe to do so, deploy a warning triangle some distance up the road to inform other motorists that danger lies ahead.

A first aid kit is now commonplace in most new cars but, if not, there are plenty on the market. They are fine for treating minor injuries. You should only administer first aid to a level you have been trained to. Also, it is recommended that you have a fire extinguisher in your car, but be aware that domestic versions will only help to knock down the very smallest of conflagrations.

Approaching the scene of an accident

Top tips
• Be alert to warning signals, including flashing lights, and be prepared to stop
• Always obey the instructions of police or Highways Agency officers
• Be sensitive to road conditions
• Watch out for emergency vehicles arriving at the accident scene
• Do not 'rubberneck'

In approaching an accident scene be mindful that the condition of the road

If it's a multi-car shunt on a major junction, like here, the accident scene can become very busy.

Crashed vehicles don't always end up on their own four wheels, causing the emergency services to adapt their techniques.

could have been a contributory factor. Standing water, ice or oil may all be present, so brake gently and carefully, and don't fall foul of the very problem that might have caught out those already involved in the original incident.

Accident scenes are dangerous places for those involved in addressing the consequences. The emergency services will need space to undertake their various responsibilities, whether attending to casualties, removing debris or eventually reopening the road. They may even have to clear a space for an air ambulance helicopter to land. There's no way of avoiding the fact that this work, of necessity, has to be carried out in the main carriageway of the road.

A range of emergency service and incident support vehicles may be involved in dealing with the problems

Space may have to be cleared for an air ambulance to land to collect a casualty.

caused by a road traffic accident. Whilst you might readily expect and can easily recognise fire engines, ambulances and police cars, doctors may arrive independently, as may staff from the Highways Agency, and in a variety of relatively unfamiliar vehicles. All will display flashing lights – whether blue, red, green or amber – accompanied by sirens, and sometimes, flashing headlights. It is in everyone's interest that they arrive speedily at the scene so let them past, which may mean moving to the side of the carriageway. In doing so, try to avoid braking harshly, mounting the kerb, or otherwise creating extra risk for other road users.

If it's possible to safely pass the accident scene, or it's on the other side of a dual carriageway, don't slow down to try to see what's happening. As well as being very distracting for you as a driver, this has frequently been the cause of additional accidents – just what the emergency services don't need.

What should I do if I happen across a road traffic accident?

Top tips
- Look after your own safety
- Obtain information about vehicles involved, the number and condition of casualties, and location
- Alert the emergency services
- Do not move a casualty unless they are in imminent danger
- Turn off the ignition of vehicles involved
- Do not smoke
- Help any casualties

If you come across a road traffic collision, you must first make sure that you look after your own safety. A serious hazard is the potential of other vehicles becoming involved and crashing into the existing wreckage, so be well aware

However small the accident it can be a shocking experience, so knowledge of what to do is both important and reassuring at what is a stressful time. (Courtesy RAC)

of this and try not to take your eyes off approaching traffic. Do not wander too close to road lanes where traffic is still flowing, and only act within your own knowledge and experience.

Initially, obtain as much information as you can including:

Number of vehicles involved
Types of vehicles, such as Heavy Goods Vehicles (HGVs), agricultural vehicles, etc
Number and condition of casualties
The precise location of the accident

You should alert the emergency services, having established as accurately as possible your exact location. If in doubt, describe any obvious landmarks to the emergency operator. The Fire Service request that you do not leave the scene until they have arrived, as sometimes vehicles may be obscured behind hedges or

in fields and are not always obvious. Anyway, the police may well want to ask you for witness information too.

The temptation might be to try to remove people from a crashed vehicle, but it's crucial that they should first be assessed by a paramedic before being moved. The only exception is if the car is on fire, or there is an imminent risk of further injury.

If in any doubt, do not put yourself at risk, instead phone the emergency services, giving as much detail as possible.

What if I'm involved in an accident?

Should you be involved in a road collision yourself, which is defined by *The Highway Code* as resulting, "… in damage or injury to any other person, vehicle, animal or property," you are required by The Road Traffic Act to do the following:

Can I drive my car? An experienced assessment after an accident is undoubtedly beneficial. (Courtesy RAC)

You must stop at the scene

You should be prepared, as the driver, to give your name and address, as well as the name and address of the vehicle's owner – if different – as well as your vehicle's registration number to "… anyone having reasonable grounds for requiring them." This would include the police and other drivers involved. If you can't do this at the time of the incident, it is a requirement that the police are informed within 24 hours

In the case of an accident which has involved physical injury, this must be reported to the police as soon as possible, but certainly within 24 hours

You should ideally produce your insurance certificate for the police at the accident scene. If you don't have it with you it must be produced for the police within seven days

You should exchange your insurance details with interested parties

You should contact your own insurer or insurance broker and inform them immediately of what has happened

You would be well advised to take the contact details of any witnesses to the incident. When asking for a telephone number, ask for a home landline and don't rely solely on a mobile phone number. At the same time if you have a camera, maybe as part of your mobile phone, take some photographs of the accident scene to reinforce the fine detail of what has happened. Support this evidence, if you can, with some hand-written notes and a diagram of the scene as outlined in the next section.

From a legal point of view, do not admit liability for the accident, and avoid any discussions about possible causes, particularly if you feel you might have been at fault. Also avoid any apologies as these could subsequently be used against you too.

If the incident hasn't involved personal injury nor another vehicle but has damaged items such as bollards, lampposts or fences and it is unclear whether it is owned by a local council or a private landowner then you should inform the police who will in turn tell the appropriate person or authority.

What if I witness a road accident?

Top tips
- Write some descriptive notes
- Take photos
- Don't be intimidated

It's quite possible that if you have seen a road accident that you may be asked to be a witness. The information you subsequently give may be of use to the police, a solicitor or an insurance company, and probably all three.

As soon as possible, you should write down some notes and make them as full as you can whilst details are clear in your mind. Include a sketch of the accident scene showing where vehicles ended up, and the directions in which they were originally travelling. It's easy with camera phones to take supporting pictures too to substantiate your notes. Just make sure you don't put yourself at risk from other traffic at the accident scene when trying to capture the relevant photographic angles.

Your notes and supporting photos should show:

Weather and road conditions
The layout, names and widths of the roads
The positioning of all the vehicles involved
The location of road markings, traffic signs
Details of any skid marks and locations of broken glass
Estimated speed of the vehicles involved

After an accident, while your memory is clear, note down the details of what has happened including the positioning of the vehicles concerned – before and after the accident.

If you have a camera take as many photographs as possible or, more likely, use your camera phone. Hang on to the evidence.

seven
Fire safety

Every year there are about 35,000 accidental vehicle fires in the UK, with most being the result of poor maintenance and car defects. Only about 7% are as a result of road traffic accidents, so most could have been prevented.

Car fires should be treated with great respect. It takes much more than a domestic fire extinguisher to deal with such a blaze.

Top tips
• Check the vehicle's electrical wiring for signs of damage or wear. Any additions or alterations should be carried by a qualified vehicle electrician
• Check the fuel lines for wear and that the connections are secure
• Don't weld or use any heat source near the fuel tank or pipes
• Place a foam or dry powder fire extinguisher in your car that conforms to BS EN3

What should I do if a fire breaks out?

Top tips
• Stop the car
• Switch off engine
• Release bonnet – **do not open**
• Get everyone out of the vehicle and move them away – keep onlookers away too
• Dial 999 and ask for the Fire and Rescue Service

- Warn oncoming traffic, if safe to do so
- Use a dry powder or foam extinguisher (BS EN3) if safe to do so. Do not open the bonnet if the fire is in the engine compartment. Aim the extinguisher under the edge of the bonnet
- If in doubt, don't tackle the fire – leave it to the Fire and Rescue Service
- Never use water on an engine fire – it may short out electrical wiring and spread burning petrol

If faced with a car fire in any situation, and not necessarily an accident, you should maintain a safe distance, having moved yourself and others to a safe location. Wait for the Fire Service to arrive. As a rule of thumb, you shouldn't intervene, as fighting this type of fire can lead to injuries and burns if you are not trained.

Be aware that apart from the obvious fuel source there are hazards, such as gas struts that hold a car's bonnet open that will explode when subjected to heat. Also be alert to the fact that when air bags are deployed in an accident, a powder is released into the air that sometimes makes people believe the car is on fire when it is not.

A fuel fire can develop with speed, and if there is a large spill this can become a running fuel fire, which is when the fuel is burning as it moves along the ground. Such fires need to be extinguished by trained personnel with the use of sizeable foam or dry powder extinguishers.

The accompanying photographs illustrate a petrol fire on a motor racing circuit where the emergency services were on the spot. The series of photographs covers a period of less

Whether or not there is a fire, the fire service will deploy appropriate equipment to cope in case a late conflagration occurs.

This photo sequence is of a motor racing fire. The Aston Martin involved had a mechanical failure which ruptured a fuel line.

In a matter of seconds a running fire erupted whilst the driver drew to a halt and leaped out.

Trained help with professional equipment was immediately available but it still took some time to knock down the fire.

The circuit's fire engine crew finally extinguished the blaze. In this case, only a small amount of fuel was involved compared to that often found in a road car.

than a minute, during which a running petrol fire is shown, the fire enveloped the driver's compartment, the driver escaped, and a fierce fire started. The fire was addressed by trained fire marshals with substantial fire equipment, but it actually took one of the circuit's fire tenders and its crew to fully extinguish the blaze, even though it involved a relatively small quantity of petrol, and there was little in the way of flammable seats or carpets to contribute to the fire.

What happens when the Fire Service arrives?

The Fire Service will approach the incident at a controlled speed to assess the situation as they arrive. Depending on how big the incident is, they may park some distance away to avoid any debris if there has been an accident.

Fire Service priorities will be scene safety, closure of the road, the fire fighting media they need, the assessment of casualties and their triage (the identification of those in most need of immediate medical attention) and treatment.

The officer in charge will do a 360-degree assessment of the scene. In doing this, he/she will identify all hazards, such as exposed electricity cables from damaged lamp posts, walls in danger of collapsing, and other potential difficulties. The fire crew will set up their fire fighting equipment as a control measure, even if there is no initial fire. Fire crews are

One reason to keep clear of a fire. Gas struts, which are found in several places on cars, can explode, missile-like, in a fire.

If a casualty in a car accident complains of back or neck pain the car's roof must come off using powerful cutters like this.

all first-aid trained and in some cases to a higher level so they may take over the care of a casualty or assist the paramedics where needed.

The fire crew will carry out a casualty-centred rescue having created a safer environment than when they arrived. One aim is to neutralise the vehicles themselves so, amongst other precautions, the ignitions are turned off. There is a specific problem with some electric hybrids in that as they are often silent, the engine can still be live, and a threat to both the casualty and the emergency personnel. In such situations, the Fire Service should be given the ignition key.

The car's roof is removed, ensuring it's kept clear of the casualty.

The spinal board can now be inserted behind the casualty to minimise the possibility of aggravating any injuries.

The casualty is removed safely with his head supported by a member of the extrication team.

The Fire Service's aim is to bring any chaos under control and to maintain everyone's safety during the incident.

What if a car's driver or passengers are trapped?

The Fire Service will use a casualty-centred approach. This means anything it does must not aggravate the casualty's injuries or cause further injury or discomfort. However, there is one exception, and this is if there is an immediate threat to the casualty's life. Then the casualty will have to be moved and, whilst this might affect their condition, this is acceptable in such a critical situation. During extraction a spinal board will be used. This is a stretcher-like handling device which provides rigid support during the movement of a casualty with suspected spinal or limb injuries. Whilst the casualty is being moved in this way, an open airway must be maintained at all times.

A cautionary note from the Fire Service. When a casualty has been in an accident the initial rush of adrenaline may mask the pain of injury. On one occasion a casualty felt well enough to get out of the crashed vehicle unaided and a passer-by then sat him in his own car. After a while, back pain became evident to such an extent that the Fire Service was obliged to remove the roof of the otherwise undamaged Good Samaritan's car, to allow the casualty to be safely transferred on a spinal board to the waiting ambulance ...

eight
Roadside first aid

Top tips
- Look after your own safety
- DO NOT move any casualties unless they are in imminent danger
- DO NOT give casualties food or drink
- DO reassure casualties and make them comfortable
- Administer emergency first aid as necessary and within your capabilities

First aid is by definition the administration of emergency medical treatment to injured persons in that period before the arrival of paramedics. A sound knowledge of the basics of first aid – ideally coming from your first aid training – can be invaluable in the eventual recovery of an accident victim.

Emergency 999 phone calls to the ambulance service are prioritised to make sure that those cases that are life-threatening receive the quickest possible response. It is usual for 75% of such calls to be responded to within eight minutes and 95% will receive an

ambulance that can transport a casualty to hospital within 19 minutes.

In a road accident situation you should always dial 999 if anyone is seriously injured, and their life might be at risk. Once connected to an ambulance emergency operator you will be asked a series of questions to establish the seriousness of the situation. This helps the ambulance

The ambulance service aims to attend 75% of life-threatening incidents within eight minutes. First aid may prove indispensable until paramedics arrive.

service dispatch an appropriate response as soon as possible. You should not hang up but await a response from the ambulance control room as it might need to ask you extra questions. It might be that it can give you advice on what to do in the way of first aid until a paramedic reaches the scene.

If you come across a road accident you should park safely and in a position that puts your vehicle out of risk, and where it will not impede the emergency services when they arrive. Make sure you have turned off your car's engine. Switch on your car's hazard warning lights, put on your reflective jacket, and deploy your hazard triangle if it safe to do so. Signal to other traffic, but don't stand in the middle of the road; rather stay on the side of the road and, if appropriate, on the pavement. Assess the situation calmly.

Medical emergencies on the road can involve anything from a single casualty to a number of casualties, some of whom who may even be trapped in separate vehicles. You should first ensure that it is actually safe for you to administer first aid at the site of the accident. Would you be personally at risk if you approach the vehicle in the fast carriageway of a busy road, for example? Are there hazards, such as broken glass, fuel leaks, and fast approaching traffic?

If it is safe you should assess whether or not anybody involved is in imminent danger. Watch out, especially for casualties who are quiet. They may be unconscious and may be at more risk than those who are obviously bleeding and very vocal. Ensure that the emergency services have been called, or do this first, if not.

Administering first aid

It's absolutely imperative that casualties aren't moved from their vehicles unless there is a risk to them, such as the car catching fire. Moving them unnecessarily and in the wrong way could aggravate existing injuries

Crash scenes can be difficult for the ambulance service to operate in due to the proximity of passing traffic.

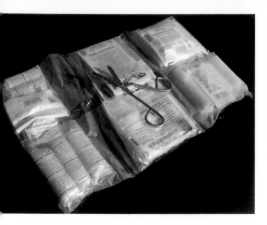

First aid kits in some cars (here BMW) can be used to treat most minor injuries.

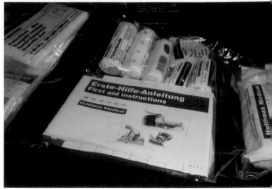

Instructions will come with most first aid kits, but it's better to be fully trained to know how to use the contents effectively.

and even, amongst other potential problems, cause paralysis.

If the casualty is a motorcyclist do not remove his/her helmet unless it is absolutely essential, such as where their airway is blocked or they are not breathing and need cardiopulmonary resuscitation (CPR), commonly known as 'the kiss of life' and involves chest compressions (see DRABC).

It is very possible that people involved in a road accident will be in shock. Symptoms of shock might include pale grey skin colour, rapid shallow breathing, sweating, and a rapid pulse. Bleeding from a wound can cause the onset of shock. A person in shock should not be given any food or liquids. You can make them comfortable, which includes keeping them warm, using extra clothing or a space/survival wrap emergency blanket. Do not move them unnecessarily. If their situation allows lie them down, keep them warm and raise their legs. It's recommended that you reassure the casualty, and, if appropriate, hold their hand, which will give great comfort.

You should recognise that even if a person involved in a road accident is mobile, they have been in a traumatic situation and may well be disorientated. They should, therefore, not be left on their own to wander around a crash scene where there may be the extra danger to them of passing traffic.

Emergency first aid – DRABC

D – Make sure you are not in DANGER
R – Ask the casualty some questions to try and obtain a RESPONSE
A – We all need to be able to breathe. We do this through our AIRWAY which is our mouth and nose. It is essential that all casualties should have a clear airway which needs to be kept open. Gently open the airway by tilting their head back and gently lifting their chin.
B – The casualty should be BREATHING normally, and this should be checked by looking for chest rise and fall and listening and feeling for breath – abnormal breathing may be a sign of cardiac arrest and an indication to start CPR.
C – Should the casualty not be breathing CHEST COMPRESSIONS are needed. This is known as CPR (Cardiopulmonary

71

Resuscitation). Compressions involve placing your hands, one on top of the other, in the middle of the patient's chest – in between the armpits and pressing down 5-6cm then releasing. This procedure should be repeated between a 100 and 120 times per minute. The recommendation is that 30 compressions should be given, and then, having tilted the casualty's head back, pinch their nose and then blow into the patient's mouth for about a second, and repeat – it should take no more than five seconds to deliver the two breaths. Repeat the procedure of 30 compressions and two breaths until breathing and consequent circulation is restored.

The same procedure can be carried out for children who are not breathing normally, although there are a couple of alterations that will help to make it more effective. If the child is not breathing normally, attempt ventilation prior to carrying out CPR and the compression depth should be at least one third of the depth of the chest, or about 4cm.

If the casualty is bleeding, the medical advice is to place pressure on the wound to stem the flow of blood. Ideally use a dressing from a first aid kit, but if none is handy a clean piece of material will do.

Do make sure, though, that you do not aggravate the wound if there are glass or metal shards present, which is quite possible in an accident situation. Apply a dressing to the wound and fasten in place with a bandage.

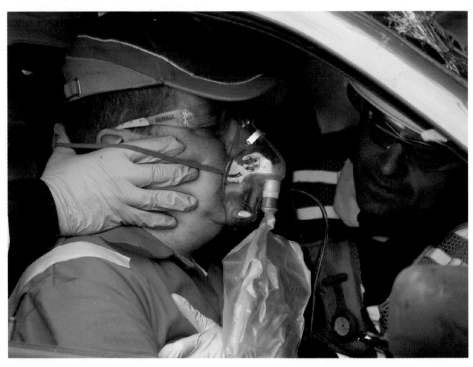

Here the Fire Service maintains the crash driver's head position and his airway whilst assessing his overall situation and condition.

The recovery position can be used to protect an unconscious but breathing casualty from choking by keeping their airway open.

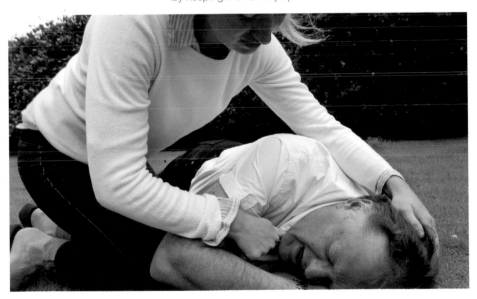

In the recovery position the casualty's head is gently tilted backwards, to maintain an airway, and downwards, to allow any fluids to drain out.

In a situation where the casualty has suffered burns, the safest solution is, if available, to use cool, clean running water to cool the injury, ideally for a minimum of ten minutes. Leave in place anything that might be sticking to the burn.

First aid kit

The contents of a typical first aid kit – such as those pictured – which was supplied new with the car, contains both small and large plastic adhesive strips, sterile gauze pads, stretch gauze, various sizes of sterile bandage dressings, roll gauze, triangular bandage, safety pins, a survival wrap emergency blanket, adhesive tape, a first aid Instruction booklet, and a pair of scissors.

Always carry a first aid kit.

To be certain you are able to help effectively in an accident situation you should undertake first aid training, which could also prove crucial in other situations and not necessarily just on the road.

Emergency first aid training may be obtained from a qualified organisation, such as your local Ambulance Trust. In addition, the British Red Cross and the St John Ambulance organisations offer training as does St Andrews First Aid in Scotland.

RAC the driving people

Caring for your car
How to maintain & service your car

Trevor Fry

ISBN: 978-1-845843-96-0 • Paperback
21x14.8cm • £9.99* UK/$19.95* USA
96 pages • 177 colour pictures

RAC the driving people

Caring for your car's bodywork and interior

Simon Nixon

ISBN: 978-1-845843-88-5 • Paperback
21x14.8cm • £9.99* UK/$19.95* USA
80 pages • 115 colour pictures

RAC the driving people

Caring for your scooter
How to maintain & service your 49cc to 125cc twist & go scooter

Trevor Fry

ISBN: 978-1-845840-95-2 • Paperback
21x14.8cm • £9.99* UK/$19.95* USA
80 pages • 89 colour pictures

RAC the driving people

Caring for your bicycle
Your expert guide to keeping your bicycle in tip-top condition

Peter Henshaw

ISBN: 978-1-845844-77-6 • Paperback
21x14.8cm • £6.99* UK/$11.99* USA
64 pages • 97 colour pictures

For more info on Veloce titles, visit our website at www.veloce.co.uk
email: info@veloce.co.uk • Tel: +44(0)1305 260068
* prices subject to change, p&p extra

ISBN: 978-1-845843-90-8 • Paperback
21x14.8cm • £12.99* UK/$24.95* USA
104 pages • 92 colour and b&w pictures

ISBN: 978-1-845844-94-3 • Paperback
21x14.8cm • £9.99* UK/$19.99* USA
80 pages • 86 colour pictures

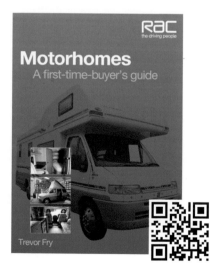

ISBN: 978-1-845844-49-3 • Paperback
21x14.8cm • £9.99* UK/$19.95* USA
80 pages • 109 colour and b&w pictures

ISBN: 978-1-845844-95-0 • Paperback
21x14.8cm • £9.99* UK/$19.95* USA
80 pages • 95 colour pictures

For more info on Veloce titles, visit our website at www.veloce.co.uk
email: info@veloce.co.uk • Tel: +44(0)1305 260068
* prices subject to change, p&p extra

Index